ENHANCE YOUR QUILTS—
EMBELLISH!

TERRY WHITE

◆ American Quilter's Society
P. O. Box 3290 • Paducah, KY 42002-3290
www.AmericanQuilter.com

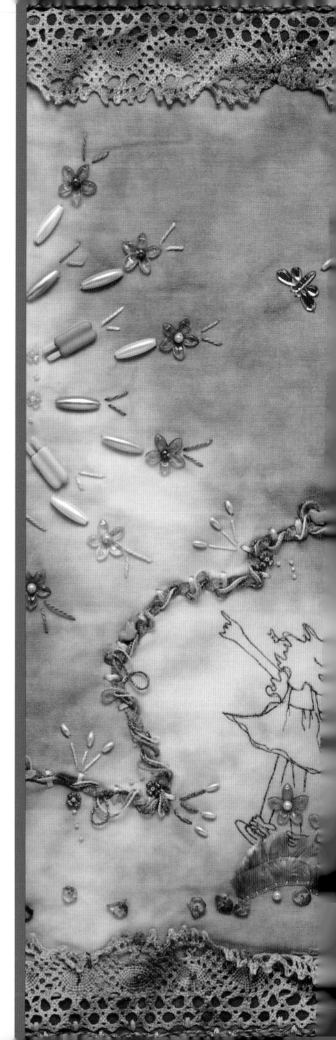

Located in Paducah, Kentucky, the American Quilter's Society (AQS) is dedicated to promoting the accomplishments of today's quilters. Through its publications and events, AQS strives to honor today's quiltmakers and their work and to inspire future creativity and innovation in quiltmaking.

EXECUTIVE BOOK EDITOR: ANDI MILAM REYNOLDS
SENIOR EDITOR: LINDA BAXTER LASCO
COPY EDITOR: CHRYSTAL ABHALTER
GRAPHIC DESIGN: MELISSA POTTERBAUM
COVER DESIGN: MICHAEL BUCKINGHAM
PHOTOGRAPHY: CHARLES R. LYNCH
ADDITIONAL PHOTOGRAPHY: TERRY WHITE

American Quilter's Society
P. O. Box 3290 • Paducah, KY 42002-3290
www.AmericanQuilter.com

Additional copies of this book may be ordered from the American Quilter's Society, PO Box 3290, Paducah, KY 42002-3290, or online at www. AmericanQuilter.com.

Text © 2011, Author, Terry White
Artwork © 2011, American Quilter's Society

LIBRARY OF CONGRESS CATALOGING-IN-PUBLICATION DATA

White, Terry, 1956 June 5-
   Enhance your quilts : embellish! / by Terry White.
      p. cm.
   ISBN 978-1-60460-009-4
   1. Quilting. I. Title.
   TT835.W497 2011
   746.46--dc23
                        2011025359

TITLE PAGE: SUN AND BLUES, detail. Full quilt on page 29.

THIS PAGE AND OPPOSITE: SUN POPS, detail. Full quilt on page 68.

DEDICATION

This book is dedicated to the most happy memories of my lovely grandmothers:

Grandma Blanche opened up the wonderful world of flea markets and sparked my love for vintage stuff.

Nana inspired my use of shiny things with fabric with her fabulous costume making.

The least I can do is pass it on!

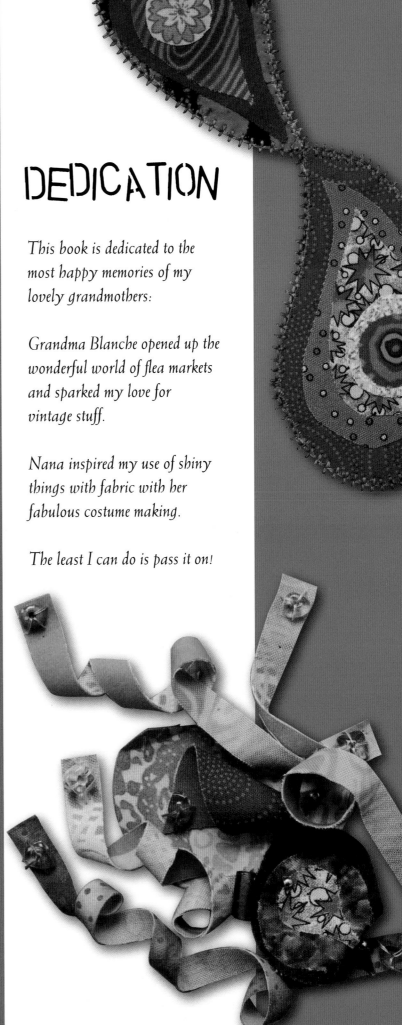

ACKNOWLEDGMENTS

Writing a book is hard for me (really hard!) but I love this part where I can thank people! I am so appreciative of the editors and designers of the American Quilter's Society!

Thank you Linda Baxter Lasco, my great editor. You are a good friend; you are patient and understanding of my quirky ways. You get the gold star*! Thank you Andi Reynolds—you are an amazing encourager, so organized, and an all-around lovely person. Thank you Melissa Potterbaum for designing a lovely book from my piles of needlework. Thank you Charley Lynch for your outstanding photography, which always makes my stuff look good. Thank you Michael Buckingham for the really cool cover for this book—I'm thrilled with it.

I would like to thank the people in the stitching industry for their constant encouragement and support.

Nancy Jewell, Lynn Brown, Ken Nelson (Coats & Clark), Jeannine Delpit (BERNINA), Patrick Carothers, Bev Crone (Havel's Scissors), Liz Kettle, Kathy Stull, Pokey Bolton, Helen Gregory, and Penny McMorris—encouragers and all-around wonderful people.

Thank you to my husband, Scot—love, friend, and constant companion.

Thank you, thank you, thank you all!

Terry White

THIS PAGE AND OPPOSITE: SPRING TOTEM, detail. Full quilt on page 63.

TABLE OF CONTENTS

INTRODUCTION

"Embellishmentality" is a frame of mind and a way to work. We see something good and if something is added, it becomes better. We see two different things that are good and if we combine them, we get a third thing that is better than either one of the first two things.

I don't have hard and fast rules for the design work with embellishments. Big or small, high contrast or low—the important thing is that the design enhances the embellishments and the embellishments enhance the design.

APPROACHES TO DESIGN

Some of the ideas I explore in my work are listed here:

Everything in nature is made of small parts. The small parts can be very beautiful. Beads are seeds, bugs, and rocks. Buttons become flowers and animals. Yarns are vines. Lace and pearls remind me of a beach.

Break down a design into its small parts, then combine small things to make the quilt.

Begin with a design or a pattern and develop it with combinations of techniques and embellishments.

DOMESTIC CAT, made by the author

In this simple design repetition is used with alterations in size and line. To quilters, repetition as a design idea is not new.

Isolate and enhance a design to make it the focal point and show its importance, as in a medallion design.

Pull out some of your UFOs (unfinished objects). LOOKING THROUGH THE BLUES brings together parts of five different unfinished projects. As I played with the parts, I began to look at the projects in a whole new way.

LOOKING THROUGH THE BLUES, **made by the author**

GOT STUFF?

Enhance a design with embellishments to re-enforce its beauty. A clear, clean design can be enriched with color and texture. My tendency is to group analogous colors. The textures I choose remain consistent within the design. For example, use tightly wound threads and shiny solid color beads for strong graphic designs.

Choose simple techniques for big effects.

Playtime promotes free-association that can lead to interesting combinations of materials. Sometimes, just playing with my materials (you can call it "organizing" or "cleaning") can spark an idea for a new quilt.

INFLUENCE—THE FLOW OF IDEAS

I do a variety of things to realize my ideas as art. I'm in the process of "making" all the time. This gives me a cross-reference of ideas and causes my media to be mixed.

Inspiration comes to me from doing. Gardening is a perfect example of this. The idea of using a bar tack for stitching down a yarn and then wrapping it with ribbon came from pulling vines out of a rosebush. Knots in a brown yarn look like the little twigs I find under our trees.

To move forward with an idea sometimes requires inspiration from other people. I learn techniques and gather ideas from books, classes, and videos.

MY GOALS FOR YOU

I hope this book will:

+ Help you see your materials in a new light.
+ Be a reference of techniques.
+ Assist you with color choices.
+ Be inspirational.
+ Encourage you to experiment.
+ Encourage you to explore your own art with simple techniques for getting it done.

Sometimes, we don't know what process to use to accomplish an artistic idea. Often we think, "I don't know if it is okay to do it this way." All techniques that artists use were made up by people. There is no one "right way." If it works for you, then it is right!

The techniques I share may spark a way to use things that I haven't covered. You may find a tiny thing in one corner of this book that you can expand on to make a whole new thing. I hope you do!

THE TECHNICALITIES OF FUN

This title doesn't even sound right! How can you have fun if you are concerned about technicalities? Well, the truth is that if you've got the technical aspects right, then you are free to have all the fun in the world with your sewing machine.

KNOW YOUR SEWING MACHINE

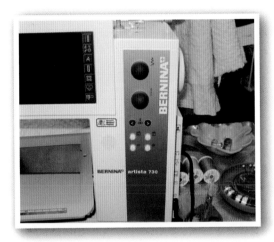

The manual that comes with your sewing machine is an essential tool for learning how to use it and finding out all the things it is capable of doing. Keep your machine clean and in good working order. The tension system on your machine can wear out or move out of alignment over time, so getting your machine serviced regularly is important. I use a BERNINA and I call her Sally. We are best friends forever (BFFs).

THREAD DELIVERY

Thread delivery refers to the way the thread comes off the spool before it goes through the first thread guide on the sewing machine. This is the first thing that can affect the tension of the thread.

We have an amazing variety of decorative threads available to us. We need to understand that they all don't work like regular sewing threads in our machines. Some threads will require adjustments to the thread delivery. For basic sewing, use your machine's horizontal spool pin. Some machines include an upright spool pin. Add a good thread stand to your sewing station and you should have thread delivery covered.

Threads labeled "Machine Quilting" may be cross-wound or straight-wound. These terms refer to the way that threads are wound onto the cone or spool. Cross-wound threads work well on a thread stand where they are pulled up; straight wound threads should be pulled from the side.

A heavy spool can create more tension on the thread, so sitting in on a spool cup on the upright pin can help the spool move more freely.

The Technicalities of Fun

When working with metallic threads (especially the flat ones) and very lightweight spools, using an upright pin and pulling from the side prevents the threads from twisting and breaking. Add a felt pad under the spool to add friction and keep the thread from whirling off the spool.

A very lightweight spool can move too fast and get caught up in the tension discs and knot up. So I use a felt or foam spool pad to add friction to the light spool.

When sewing decorative stitches, always stitch at an even, steady speed. Stitching too fast can add tension to the thread and ruin a pretty stitch.

When I bring home a new group of threads, the first thing I do is to test them. I put them through their paces with thread painting, quilting, and decorative stitching. This gives me a chance to see their properties, determine the best delivery system, and decide which tension settings to use. Then, I know how beautifully they will work when I choose them for a specific project.

TENSION SETTINGS

Over the years I've heard some people say that they were told to never "mess with" their tension settings. People who stitch a lot always change their tension settings. You wouldn't stitch on silk chiffon with the same settings used to stitch on heavy wool. So learning about the tensions on your machine is very important.

Loose tension—When you lower the number on the top thread tension, you are opening the tension discs. This loosens the tension and allows the top thread (which goes through the needle) to move more freely through the discs.

Tight tension—When you raise the number on the top tension, you are closing the tension discs. This tightens the tension, which adds friction to the top thread and, in turn, tightens the stitch.

The tension for decorative stitches should be at a lower setting than for regular sewing. Decorative stitches should rise up on the surface of the fabric, so I generally loosen the top tension when using decorative stitches. When stitching over yarn or cording, the stitch tension should be lower and the stitch width set wider so that the thread can travel the greater distance with ease.

THE BOBBIN CASE

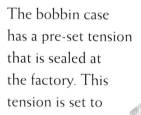

The bobbin case has a pre-set tension that is sealed at the factory. This tension is set to work with the programs on the sewing machine. The bobbin tension can be changed simply by using a thinner thread (for looser tension) or a thicker thread (for tighter tension) in the bobbin.

I have a second bobbin case for my machine (shown at left) that I use when I want to change the tension for a specific thread. It has a screw that I can loosen or tighten to change the amount of tension on the bobbin thread.

SEWING MACHINE NEEDLES

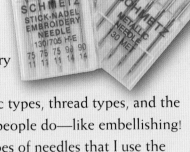

The variety of sewing machine needles is necessary because of the multitude of fabric types, thread types, and the kind of stitching people do—like embellishing! These are the types of needles that I use the most.

Machine Embroidery size 90/14
The point is sharp and the needle lasts a long time. I have a preference for thick threads or mixing two threads at once, so this larger-eyed needle works great.

Microtex
This is a fine needle with very sharp point that works well with batik fabric, silk dupioni, and micro fibers.

Metallic
Designed for use with metallic threads, this needle features a large eye and has a coating that reduces friction between the thread and the needle.

SCISSORS

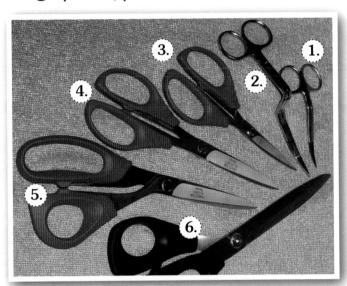

Good sharp scissors make life better. I have several pairs that are "must haves" for my work. I use Havel's scissors. They are made of the best metal alloy for scissors.

1. Multi-angled pointed tip embroidery scissors: These tiny embroidery scissors cut cleanly and very close to the fabric surface. I use them for cutting threads, yarns, and small fiber pieces. They assist in cutting the tiniest points in appliqué shapes.

2. 5¼" multi-angled embroidery scissors: This pair stays by my sewing machine all the time. There is little danger of cutting fabric when using these with decorative stitches and thread painting. The size of the finger holes makes them comfortable to use.

3. 5½" curved tip with a very fine sharp point: I use these for snipping yarns and fabric and the curve prevents snipping into the fabric. I use these for handwork and to cut most of my appliqué shapes. The curve is especially good for cutting out curved appliqué shapes.

4. 7" shears with serrated blade: This is for cutting slippery fabric and multiple layers because the really fine teeth bite into and control the fabric as you cut. They are a nice size for cutting patchwork.

5. 8" shears: For cutting large shapes, clothing, and home dec projects.

6. Professional large shears: For the really big stuff like upholstery fabric and thick layers of fabric.

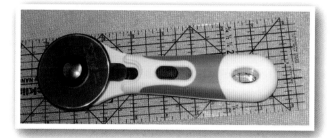

Where would we be without our rotary cutters? Well, we would be in the past before 1979! It is a really good idea to learn the proper way to use this great tool and to stay safe. You can get a good demonstration from people at quilt shows, in quilt shops, and from quilt teachers.

STITCH BASE

The stitch base is the surface or fabric combination on which you will stitch. The foundation for an embellished quilt has to be substantial enough to hold all the things you plan to add to the work. This can mean adding a firm interfacing to the back of a linen handkerchief or lightweight fabric, such as a craft stabilizer, or adding several layers of interfacing.

Open-weave fabrics like a loosely woven silk, wool, or monks cloth (linen) need a woven stabilizer to provide a solid structure for the stitching. Sometimes I will use a colored cotton or organza as a stabilizer because the stabilizer's color may show through an open weave. This can add an interesting depth of color to the work.

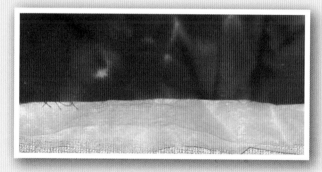

Fabrics can affect the behavior of a thread or a stitch. Here are two examples:

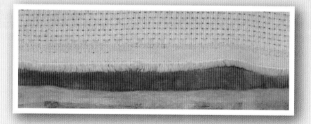

If you are stitching on a very tightly woven fabric like a batik or silk dupioni, the stitches may pucker or pull at the fabric. Using a Microtex needle, open stitches, and thin thread may be the solution. When I am embellishing fabrics like this, I usually make a separate embellishment and stitch it to the fabric.

Bonded batting with no scrim will not hold the stitching; it will eventually pull away. When stitching embellishments to your quilt, before you quilt put a lightweight woven interfacing, cheesecloth, etc. to make your own scrim. This added woven base will be a structure for the stitching.

STABILIZERS

A most frequently asked question is, "What type of stabilizer do you use?" I usually answer, "Yes." I almost always use stabilizer, but the type varies with the type of fabric and techniques used. The stabilizer may be chosen for the qualities it adds to the work.

A stabilizer:

✛ Helps to keep a fabric from distorting or puckering by adding body to a lightweight fabric.

✛ Adds thickness to the fabric to keep the bobbin thread from coming up to the top surface.

✛ Adds structure when there is none. For example, the bonded fibers of felt have no structure, so the threads will eventually distort or break down the felt. By adding a woven interfacing, the stitches have a structure to wrap around that prevents disintegration of the felt.

✛ Adds color to a sheer fabric.

✛ Prevents distortion of an embroidery on knit and twill fabrics.

✛ Does not add any stiffness when a lightweight knit interfacing is chosen.

BITS MAP

A "bits map" is a key—a reference as to where the parts go on your design so that you can take an assemblage apart to work on the individual elements. There are three steps to creating a bits map:

First, decide on a symbol to correlate to each bit. Draw this on a little piece of paper.

As you take each bit off your stitch base, mark its place on the stitch base with the corresponding symbol. This way, you will not lose your brilliant placement of each thing.

Place each bit on a flannel board in a similar arrangement to your design. I make a flannel board by gluing a piece of flannel to heavy cardstock. I recycle old file cabinet dividers instead of buying new cardstock.

Bits Map for Nana's Cloud Basket

◎ - Orange Lace Circle

ᓚ - Green Lace Piece

ᕫ - Center Purple Lace

ᑐ - Blue Lace Piece

X - Buttons

△ - ½ Circle Disc

† - Wood Leaf Shape

◯ - Red Disc

old

W

Z

STRING THEORY

When I began to explore the decorative possibilities of the sewing machine, I wanted to find ways to use my lovely yarns, crochet cotton, embroidery floss, metallic yarns, and so on.

SEWING MACHINE THREADS

There is an incredible variety of threads available to us.

MACHINE QUILTING THREAD

I designed 24 new colors of machine quilting thread for Star. I use them for thread painting, quilting, wrapping, decorative stitching, and more. There is a lot of variety in this category of threads:

✜ The weights vary greatly from one brand to the next.

✜ The fiber content may be cotton or polyester.

✜ The variegated or multicolor threads have different color change patterns. Some have a short color change every 1"–2", some change randomly every 3"–5". The short color change gives a more mottled or confetti appearance while the long color change creates a long blending change of color.

MACHINE EMBROIDERY THREAD

There is a great variety of weights available in machine embroidery threads.
The fiber content may be rayon, silk, polyester, acrylic/wool blend, cotton or Lurex®/nylon blend (metallic).

There are variegated or multicolor threads in rayon, polyester, metallic, and cotton.

Rayon is a popular embroidery thread because of its rich color and sheen that mimics silk.

Rayon twist is a thread with two different colored threads twisted consistently throughout the spool.

Metallic threads may be flat or twisted with a nylon thread.

YARN

1. Any string that is thicker than sewing machine thread I call yarn. These are cotton yarns with lovely color blends.

NATURALS

2. Crochet cotton, jute, hemp, and bamboo are some of the natural fibers shown here. These natural fiber yarns can easily be dyed or painted, as was the green cotton yarn in the picture.

PEARL COTTON

3. Pearl cotton is used to crochet lace and for hand stitching. Pearl cotton has a tight twist and shiny appearance and comes in all colors and several weights.

METALLIC YARNS

4. Through the centuries metal embroidery threads were used for the robes of kings, queens, and religious hierarchy. Thin threads can be mixed with thick ones to blend colors and for couching.

NOVELTY AND EXOTIC YARNS

5. It would take forever to list and describe so many unique threads. The fun is in the experimentation.

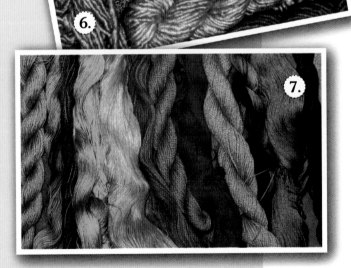

SILK

6. Silk comes in many shapes and weights; the colors are usually very rich. Silk also comes mixed with other fibers.

FLOSCHE

7. Flosche is a soft 100 percent cotton, hand embroidery yarn. It is wonderful to mix with other threads and for couching.

HOW TO MAKE YOUR OWN NOVELTY YARNS

There may be a project where you have a very specific idea of a yarn that would work, but it doesn't exist in your stitch studio. When you make cords with your own threads, then you can use the same threads in decorative stitching. This creates exciting custom combinations in your work.

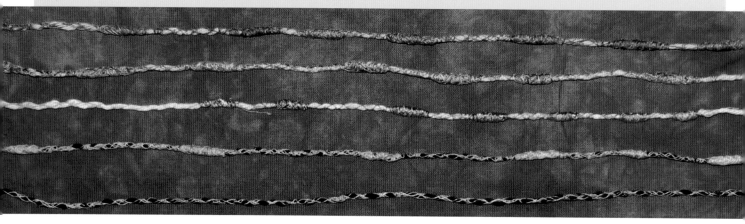

MAKE A WRAPPED CORD

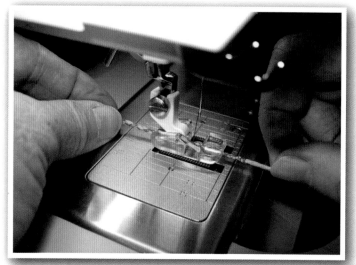

Use a cording foot and zigzag stitch. The choice of bobbin thread is important; it adds to the color and texture of the wrapped cord.

Lower the feed dogs. Use a cording and a multicolor cotton thread. Hold the cord in front and in back of the cording foot. Zigzag stitch over the cording. Pull the cord back and forth on a small section of the cord to create a bead effect with the thread. The photo shows 5 veriations

HAND-WRAPPED THREADS

Wrap threads by hand in sections over a white upholstery cord to create color blocks.

MAKE SMALL TWISTED CORDS WITH YOUR BOBBIN WINDER

1. Cut a 4 foot strand of each of the following; shiny pearl cotton, metallic thread, and three variegated sewing machine threads. In my "formula" I use 4 analogous color threads and one thread that contrasts in color with the first four.

2. Place the bobbin on the winder with the threads coming from the top of the bobbin. Hold the threads taut and turn on the bobbin winder for several seconds. Turn off the winder but don't let go of the ends. This is the first twist.

3. Holding the threads taut in one hand, find the center point of the twisted threads and hold it with your other hand.

4. Bring the end of the twisted threads to the bobbin and, holding them together, allow the twisted threads to twist together. This is the second twist, where the threads twist back onto themselves.

MAKE LARGE TWISTED CORDS WITH A SPINSTER

The Spinster (see Resources, page 94) uses the same technique as the bobbin winder, but produces bigger cords with bigger yarns and threads.

You can use everything including fabric strips and leftover ends of threads or a furry yarn.

ENHANCING THE STITCH

The sewing machine is a basic tool for the textile artist and there's a ton of potential in the variety of decorative stitches available. The idea here is to enhance the stitch with cool threads and enhance cool threads with stitches. You may have just a few decorative stitches or only utility stitches. Combine these stitches to create your own designs. Use combinations of interesting and beautiful threads for textural interest and new color ideas.

Using two threads through the eye of one needle, these threads were used to make a graduated color rainbow effect.

STITCH SAMPLERS

Keep in mind that the texture of the threads and the type and color of fabric will play a great role in this mix. Start by making stitch samples with your machine and a variety of threads. Stitching on a variety of fabric types and combinations of fabric with stabilizers is a good exercise. You will gain valuable experience and personal knowledge that you will be able to utilize in future projects.

Use the type of decorative stitches appropriate for the type of thread. All stitches don't work well with all threads. When using a thick thread, a very complicated floral stitch may end up looking like a knot (which could be very cool for some applications; it all depends on the effect you are trying to achieve). If you want the design to show, a thinner thread will show off the intricacies of the stitch.

VANILLA CRAZY, 16" x 23", made by the author

Cut squares and rectangles from a variety of fabric types. Iron them to fusible interfacing. Stitch across the many fabrics, as well as along the edges of the fabrics, as I did in this sampler.

USE TWO THREADS THROUGH THE EYE OF THE NEEDLE

Thread your sewing machine for stitching with two threads as indicated in your sewing machine manual. Instead of using a twin needle, use a 90/14 machine embroidery needle. The needle and the eye are large enough to handle two threads at once. Using two threads through the eye of the needle results in fuller stitches and a variety of great effects.

In this example, 40-wt. rayon threads were used. Each row of stitching was done with two threads at once. Changing one thread in each row results in a subtle progression of color, creating a rainbow effect. When two colors of similar hue are used (as in this example), they appear as a new color. Each time you use two threads at once, you are creating your own color twist.

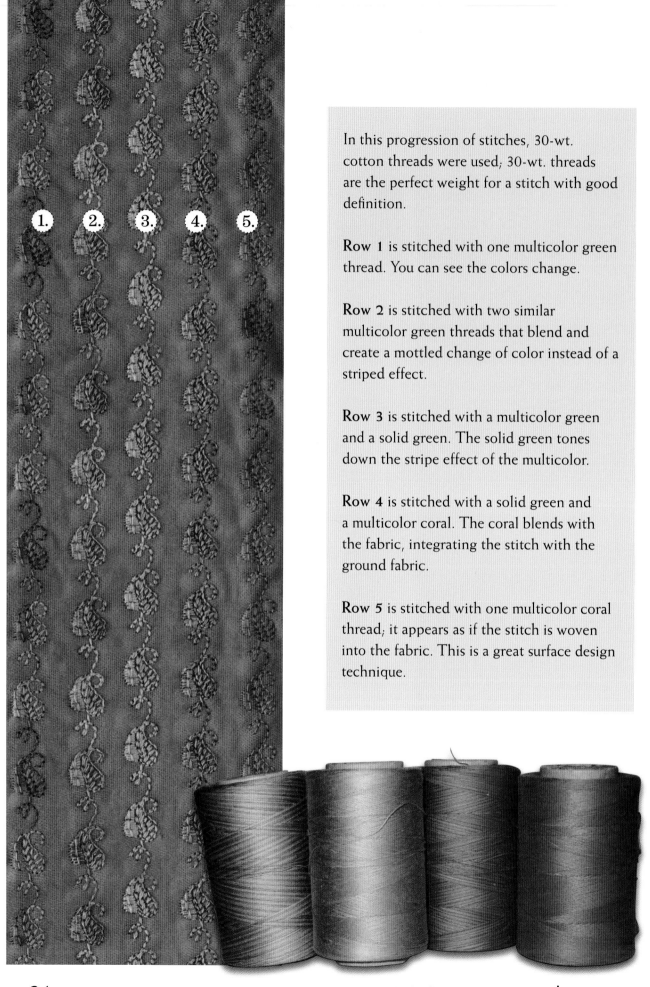

In this progression of stitches, 30-wt. cotton threads were used; 30-wt. threads are the perfect weight for a stitch with good definition.

Row 1 is stitched with one multicolor green thread. You can see the colors change.

Row 2 is stitched with two similar multicolor green threads that blend and create a mottled change of color instead of a striped effect.

Row 3 is stitched with a multicolor green and a solid green. The solid green tones down the stripe effect of the multicolor.

Row 4 is stitched with a solid green and a multicolor coral. The coral blends with the fabric, integrating the stitch with the ground fabric.

Row 5 is stitched with one multicolor coral thread; it appears as if the stitch is woven into the fabric. This is a great surface design technique.

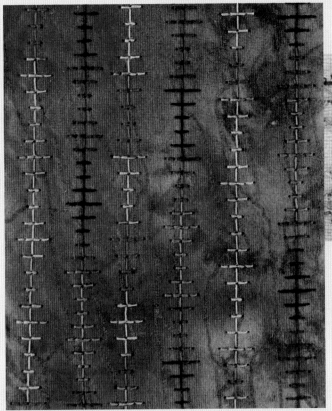

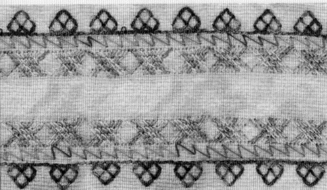

A set of three stitches is mirror-imaged. The space left between the two rows of stitches is for the insertion of a trim.

In this example one 30-wt. cotton multicolor thread is used in each row. When the colors blend with the background fabric, they "disappear." This creates a great surface design effect.

The choice of fabric affects the look of the stitching. A set of three stitches is made with the same threads on four different color fabrics. Notice the different looks achieved.

Enhancing the Stitch

1. Similar stitches are used in these two panels. The black panel looks contemporary with the red and metallic threads.

2. The pink panel is very sweet. The gold metallic stitches are done with a tailor tack foot and a zigzag stitch.

Stitches on the machine have different densities. A dense stitch has lots of close stitches to form the design. When stitched out, it makes a bold statement of color and it also draws up the fabric. Use a dense stitch in the center of a stitch set, then use more open (less dense) stitches along the sides.

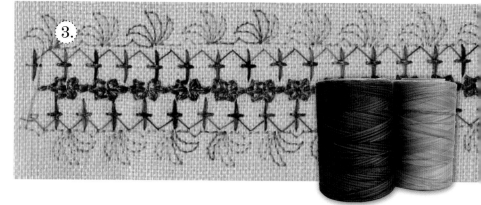

3. Use two threads in a dense stitch down the center. Use the same threads in a more open stitch down each side, then stitch outer rows with a lighter color thread and an open stitch. The more open stitches ease the puckers around the dense stitch. As seen in the sample, this process integrates the stitch set with the background fabric.

A WORD ABOUT METALLIC THREADS

When I use a flat metallic thread, I like a simple open stitch such as an open diamond. The long stitches show off the flat reflective qualities of the thread. If there are a lot of tiny stitches in the design, the needle can cut into the flat metallic thread. If I am using a complicated stitch with lots of small stitching, I'll use a twisted metallic thread.

YOU DON'T WANT YOUR STITCHING TO GO MISSING!

1. Suppose you want to make a red quilt with lots of stitching for embellishment. Red on red can be very hard to see. You want to vary the intensity of the reds and add some contrasting colored threads so you can see all your beautiful work on the quilt.

2. When you make stitch sets, if you want the stitches to line up perfectly, draw a line across the fabric and start each line of stitching at the drawn line. I must admit that I don't always do this. I like the offset look. It doesn't look perfect but I think it looks lively.

3. You can make your own trims by decorating fabric with stitches. In this sample light blue fabric was stitched, cut into strips, and pieced into a project.

BUILDING A STITCH SET TO USE AS A TRIM

1. Draw a center guideline. The foot on your machine can ride along the edge of this line.

2. Use two rose colored threads at the same time to produce a nice full diamond stitch. Add more rows of stitching with careful thread and color selection.

3. Measure and mark placement for the decorative cords. Bar tack the cords using the open appliqué foot so you can see what you're doing.

4. I used a twisted cord that I made with the same threads with which I stitched. The pink pearl cotton was also used in the twisted cord. The twisted cord is stitched down the center.

5. Here is the trim, ready to cut out and apply to my project.

SUN AND BLUES, 15½" x 25", made by the author

GREAT FEET!

This chapter is close on the heels of "Enhancing the Stitch" because they are so intertwined. It's even hard for me to do stepouts about stitches without mentioning the feet. So, I won't dance around this subject. Let's hop to and talk about our feet!

1. The multi-cord foot controls several fine yarns or cords, keeping them in order and aligning them with the center needle position for stitching. The only problem with using this foot is the tangled mess of cords feeding into it.

2. I invented a notion I call The Strand Reel, that feeds the threads off of spools on a stick that hangs around one's neck. (See Resources, page 94.) It is simple to make if you don't want to buy one.

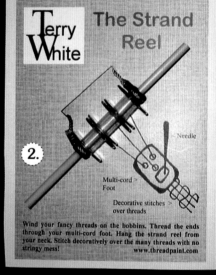

3. A cording foot controls a yarn or cord, aligning it with the center needle position for stitching.

4. A tailor tack foot creates wonderful raised stitching that looks like a caterpillar. It is used in conjunction with a wide zigzag stitch.

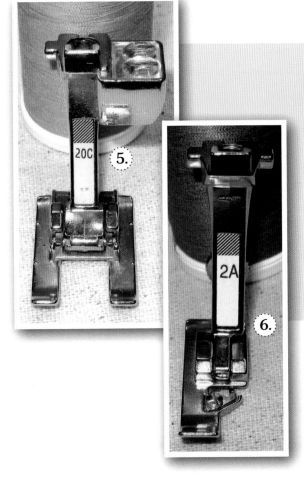

5. An open-toe appliqué foot enables you to see where you are going. If you need to follow a curved line or are stitching along the edge of an appliqué, a center needle position guide helps keep you on the line.

6. Use an overlock foot to finish the edge of a stitched motif as well as the edge of your project.

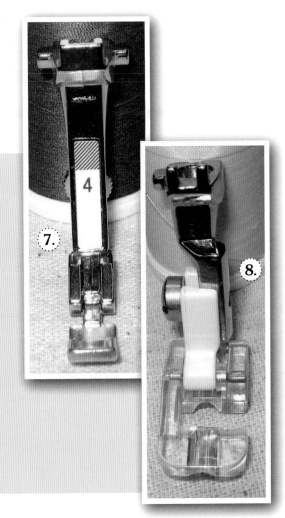

7. Use a zipper foot to stitch trims that have a woven strip along the edge (like pompom trim).

You may have many more feet available to you from your sewing machine manufacturer. It is fun to experiment with their decorative possibilities.

8. If your machine doesn't have any of these feet, check with your local quilt shop or order them online from Creative Feet (see Resources, page 93). Here is a generic cording foot from this company that fits, or can be adapted to fit, most machines.

THE GLORIES OF THE BAR TACK

The bar tack stitch on the sewing machine is a stapler for fabrics, trims, and yarns. It is great for surface embellishment. It is glorious!

LOOKING THROUGH THE BLUES, **detail (full quilt on page 33)**

The bar tack may be a stitch on your machine (check your manual) or you can use a zigzag stitch. The difference is that a programmed bar tack will stitch some small stitches to secure the stitch before and after a set number of zigzag stitches. When you use the zigzag stitch, you will have to decide when to stop stitching and if you want to secure the stitch before and after.

Here, I've used metallic thread with the bar tack to attach the crocheted rosette and the metal star to the quilt. The tack looks like a shiny bead.

LOOKING THROUGH THE BLUES, 22" x 27", made by the author

The dyed background fabric is Huck toweling with Swedish weaving embroidery on the ends. My blue cat is a recurring design with me. The blue and yellow needed red, so the cherries suddenly appeared. The key labeled "DOMESTIC" was the inspiration for the rest of the work.

DOMESTIC CATS, 15½" x 27", made by the author

CHERRY STRING

In the border treatment on DOMESTIC CATS, the tack looks like a knot in the cording (or a node on the stem).

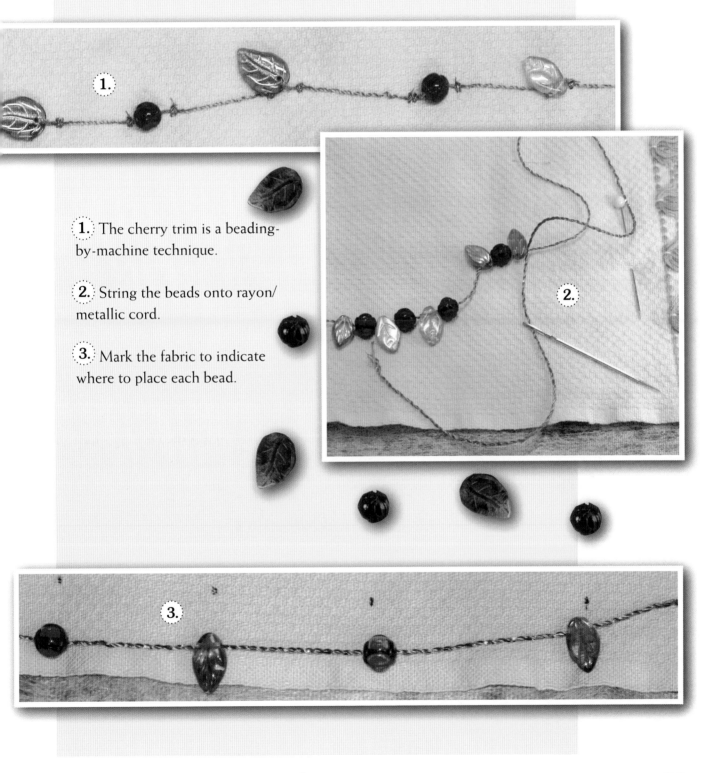

1. The cherry trim is a beading-by-machine technique.

2. String the beads onto rayon/metallic cord.

3. Mark the fabric to indicate where to place each bead.

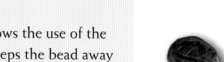

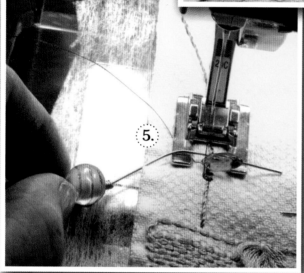

4. Bar tack to couch the string and secure the beads at the same time. Stitch in front of the bead, push it forward on the string, then stitch behind it.

5. This photo shows the use of the Beadle tool as it keeps the bead away from the needle as you stitch. (See Resources, page 94.)

WRAPPED VINE

1. An autumn mix of threads and nubby yarns makes this simple design seem more complicated to make than it is.

2. Establish the main shape of the vine with yarn and use fabric glue to secure the yarn to fabric.

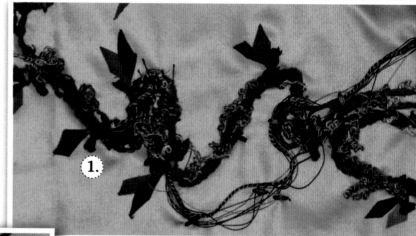

3. Add threads as you bar tack the main yarns in place.

4. Fuse small appliqué shapes along the vine.

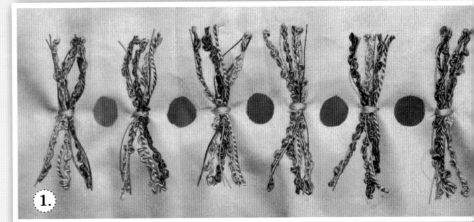

5. Lastly, thread gold yarn on a tapestry needle and wind, knot, and twist it around the central vine.

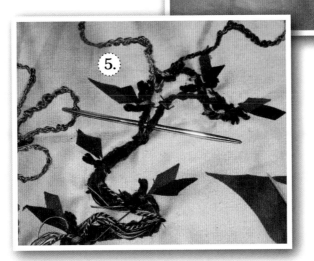

YARN BUNDLES

1. Mix several yarns and threads together to make a lovely mixed skein of yarn. Use little red ball appliqués to separate the bundles. Fuse them in place at equal intervals.

The Glories of the Bar Tack

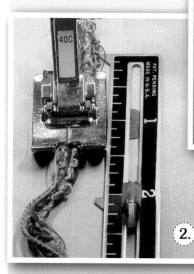

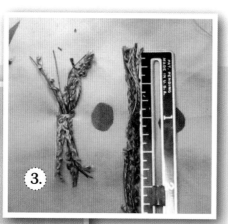

2. Use a ruler to make sure to bar tack the yarn in the center line of the trim.

3. Use the ruler again to measure where to cut the yarn to create the bundles.

CHAIN WRAP

1. Use the bar tack to stitch a decorative twist cord to the stitch base.

2. Wrap a chain around the cord between the tacks.

MULTIPLE WRAPS

Here, some yarns are bar tacked down, wrapped with other yarns, then wrapped with pearls and beads on strings. This adds dimension to the thread-painted stich base.

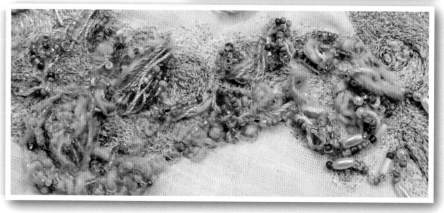

FUSED APPLIQUÉ

Fused appliqué is a versatile technique. Experiment with shapes and fabrics to get new combinations for your designs.

CHANGE A FABRIC WITH FUSED APPLIQUÉ

(**1.**) I had an old cotton blouse in with my fabrics. There were elements of the blouse I liked a lot, but I didn't like the dark green leafy thing.

(**2.**) I chose an orange fabric and fused orange seed shapes over the green things. Voila! New fabric.

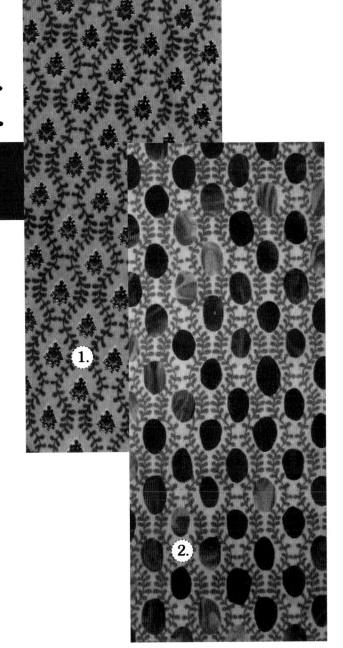

DOUBLE-FUSED FABRIC

(**1.**) For dimensional appliqué, add fusible web to the back of a fabric. Pull the release paper and fuse the fabric to the back of a contrasting fabric. You now have double-fused fabric that can be used in many ways.

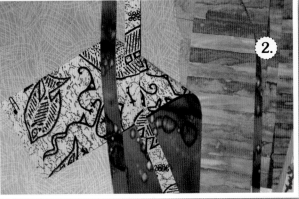

(**2.**) Long thin strips can be cut from double-fused fabric to create ribbon.

Undulant Forms is the project I am working on using this technique. I have a stabilizer underneath the fabric for a stitch base. This was laid onto a Styrofoam board. The individual pieces were cut out, twisted, and pinned in place.

The next step was to glue-tack each spot held by a pin and replace the pin. When the glue dried, I stitched them in place with a bar tack. I will add beads to the piece.

FUSE TACKS

Fabric slices with fusible web on the back can be used as "fuse tacks." They can be cut into any shape. In the examples shown, the fuse tacks repeat the colors and designs of the work in progress.

Here, the fuse tacks are simply rectangles of fused fabric holding the yarn in place.

TANGERINE, 16" x 17", made by the author

FUSED WRAPS

Apply fusible web to one side of a fabric. Fold the fabric in half and cut a shape. Open up the shape. The two halves are the exact reverse of each other. The green leaves will be wrapped around novelty yarn that looks like strings of cherries.

In this example, I stacked fused shapes before cutting out the final design. You can also see fuse tacks in the shapes of the leaves that cover spots in the yarn.

STACKED APPLIQUÉ

Add a hue of the background color to change the color just enough to highlight the embellishment. Orange cotton organdy bridges the colors of the metallic pink fabric and the lighter orange of the handkerchief.

42

3-D APPLIQUÉ

Fuse print fabrics to felt with fusible web. Felt never looked so good! Match similar colors of felt to the print.

For this piece, I simply cut out rectangles and squares, laid them out in a pleasing arrangement, and secured the pieces with fabric glue.

You can further embellish any of these appliqués with hand stitching, bar tacking, and beading.

SHADOW SHAPES

There are some tricks I use when designing with appliqué. In this sample, the black circle was too small, so I stacked it with a square of blue fabric (on the left). It didn't work, as the design was too dark. When I cut a shadow shape out of the blue fabric so that the salmon print showed through, the look was more integrated (on the right).

PLAY WITH YOUR SHAPES

1. I spent a lot of time last fall playing with color and simple forms. This shows the simplest idea.

2. The shapes were too heavy, so I split and rearranged them.

3. The third idea was to string the shapes along some knotted yarns.

I have three variations of my design concept because I took some time to play!

FABRICATIONS

HAND-WRAPPED DECORATIONS

Create a little fabric sculpture by
hand wrapping yarns and fabric
scraps with thread.

Gather elements like these.

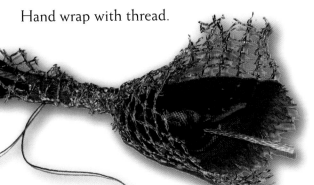

Lay out yarns and then wrap the
fabrics around them.

Hand wrap with thread.

Bury the end of the
thread into the wrap
with a tapestry needle.

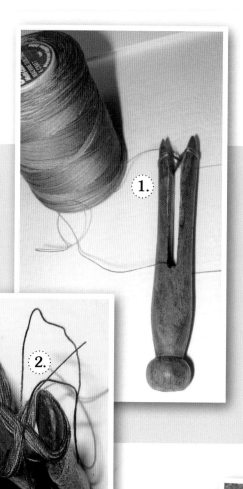

THREAD WRAPS

1. Use an old clothespin to wrap threads into bundles.

2. Lay a thread across the inside of the clothespin. This is the thread you'll use to tie off the wrap.

Wrap the threads back and forth around the clothespin in a figure-eight.

3. When the bundle is as full as you want, cut the end of the thread and tie it off.

4. Here, three thread bundles are stacked and stitched in place for each flower.

SUN-A-PILLAR, detail
(full quilt on page 48)

YO-YOS

How many ways can you use these
things? The number is infinite!
Experiment with a variety of fabrics to
see what effects you can get.

To make a yo-yo, start with a circle
of fabric. Run a line of stitching
along the edge by hand or with a big
basting stitch on the sewing machine.
Pull the thread to close the circle.
Secure with a knot.

This yo-yo is made of sparkle crinkle
organza. When making a yo-yo out
of a flimsy fabric, use dots to mark the
circle on the fabric instead of tracing.
A raspberry bead is stitched in the
center. The thread is wrapped around
the yo-yo and stitched through the
bead, drawing in the sides to make a
very fancy blossom.

I used this yo-yo on the corner of my
SUN-A-PILLAR quilt (page 48).

The idea for SUN-A-PILLAR began with chocolate and pink materials in combination with triangles. I wanted to do appliqué with metallic threads. The sun face was a "mistake" retrieved from my small parts bin.

SUN-A-PILLAR, 12" x 21½", made by the author

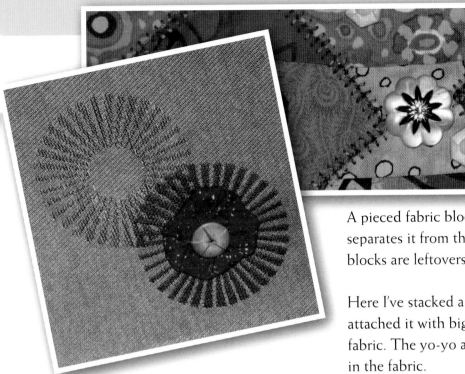

A pieced fabric block enhances this yo-yo and separates it from the background. The pieced blocks are leftovers from another project.

Here I've stacked a yo-yo with a wooden disc and attached it with big hand stitches to a decorator fabric. The yo-yo accentuates the geometric design in the fabric.

RICKRACK TWIST

Twist a dark and light rickrack to get this great barber pole effect.

COMPUTER GENERATED EMBROIDERIES

If you make stitch samples with your embroidery machine on white fabric, simply color in the background with permanent markers. Mimic the colors and print of the fabric you will be using.

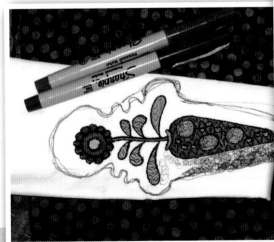

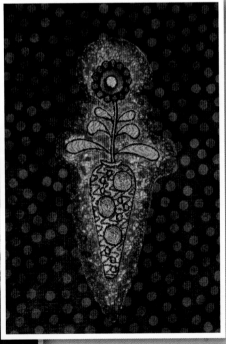

BAUBLES, BEADS, AND BUTTONS

BAUBLES

According to Webster's dictionary, a bauble is defined as a showy but worthless or useless thing; trinket, trifle, etc. "Bauble" comes from the Latin *bellus*, meaning pretty. It is true that my stitch studio is full of pretty, useless things and these make the best embellishments!

COSTUME JEWELRY

Using jewelry to richly encrust a work is so easy. A pin can simply be pinned to the work! Post earrings can be attached with the posts, just like you put them in your earlobe, (or wherever you put them). Chains can be bar tacked in a drippy fashion or twisted on a yarn wrap. I also collect broken jewelry, charms, and toy jewelry for my work.

FOUND OBJECTS

I love the term "found objects." To me it implies that one is just walking along the street and finds stuff. I work very hard to find found objects! I go to yard sales, flea markets, and second hand stores. I am also at the receiving end of family members' castoffs.

My stash of found objects includes electrical components, old hardware, toy parts, key chains, mechanical parts, and pretty much everything you might find in a junk drawer.

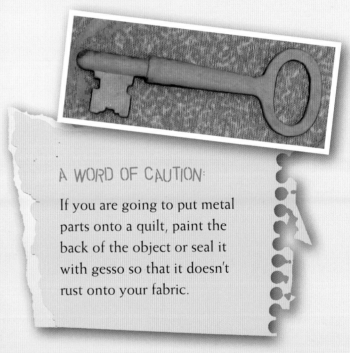

Glue game pieces to buttons so they are easy to attach to a quilt.

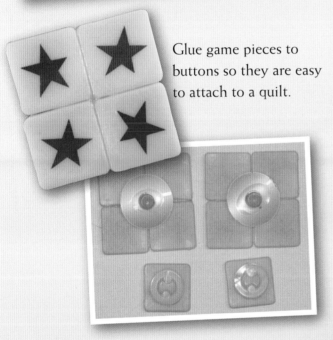

A WORD OF CAUTION:

If you are going to put metal parts onto a quilt, paint the back of the object or seal it with gesso so that it doesn't rust onto your fabric.

BEADS

Anything with a hole in it is a bead. If it needs a hole, make one!

Cut little pieces from a plastic measuring tape and a piece of blue craft foam. Use a sharp pointed crewel embroidery needle to pierce a hole in these soft materials as they are strung.

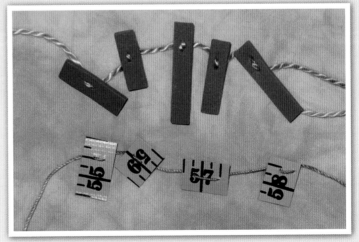

CREATE DESIGN ELEMENTS

Combine beads and trims to make embellishments that coordinate.

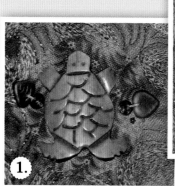

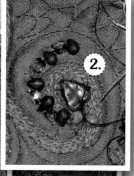

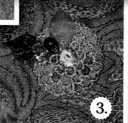

1. A circle of blue print fabric is fused to the stitch base to enhance the turtle bead with color. The turtle is flanked with bead combinations. All of this makes the turtle bead a significant design detail in the work.

2. This combination of beads makes a pretty little plant.

3. Beads are stitched over a dahlia cut from a piece of lace.

MAKE YOUR OWN BEADS

As if we don't have all the beads in the world out there, sometimes it is fun to make our own.

Use glossy magazine pages, newspapers, gift wrap, gift bags, tissue paper, or any kind of paper. This is a great recycling project.

OLD FASHIONED PAPER BEADS

2. Trace a long triangle on a piece of tracing paper. Scribble on the paper with the side of a colored pencil. Don't fill it in completely but rather layer three or four colors.

1. Colored tracing paper beads work well with hand-dyed fabrics as they have a soft changing of color.

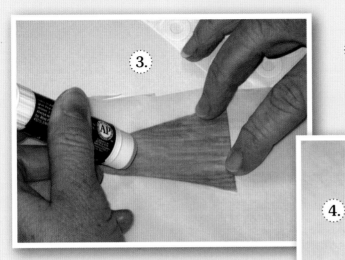

3. Cut out a triangle. Use a glue stick to spread glue over the entire uncolored side.

4. Starting at the wide end of the triangle, roll the paper onto a wooden skewer. Gently slide it off the skewer and let it dry.

FABRIC-WRAPPED BEADS

1. Start with a rectangle of fabric. Cover one side with fabric glue. Roll the fabric around a plastic straw. The color of the straw is important to the bead design because the straw stays.

2. When dry, cut the beads to desired length.

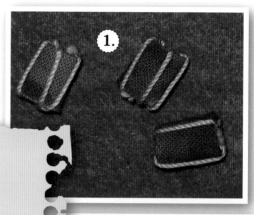

CREATIVE OPTIONS:

1. Wrap a fabric bead with decorative cords or threads.

2. Paint a fabric bead.

3. Wrap foil around a straw, then wrap it with metallic cord.

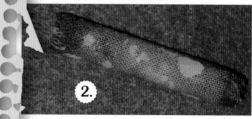

FUSED FABRIC FELT BEADS

1. For a great soft bead material, fuse fabric to both sides of a piece of felt.

2. Cut into any shape "bead" like this four-sided one. Put holes in the bead or simply use a sharp needle and stitch it in place.

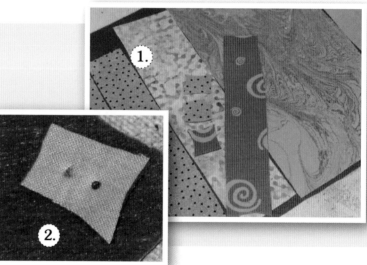

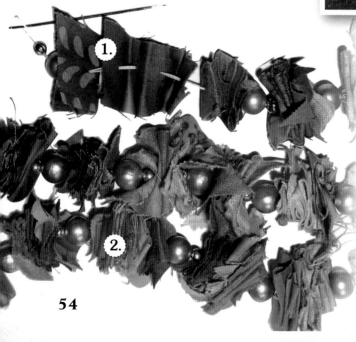

SCRAP FABRIC PLEATED "BEADS"

1. Your tiniest scraps and strips of fabric are potential beads, and it's the easiest thing to do! Cut scraps into strips of fairly consistent size. String the scraps onto a needle, folding the fabric back and forth to make pleats.

2. String pearls and metal spacers in between color groupings. This embellishment can be stitched by hand or bar tacked onto a stitch base.

THE COLLECTION, 16" x 19", made by the author

This assemblage includes a white button collection and some of my own tatted lace. This work shows the effectiveness of combining highly textured white materials.

BUTTONS

SPECIAL BUTTONS

Use your best, special buttons. If you don't, someday somebody else will find them in a yard sale and use them instead of you. Really!

You may have a really special button—lovely or sentimental—that is just not big enough to make a statement on its own. Enlarge and enhance it with embellishment techniques.

Buttons, pins, and beads enhance appliqué shapes.

Unify diverse buttons by treating them in the same manner. The buttons in the corners of SPRING TOTEM were stacked with purple yo-yos.

SPRING TOTEM detail
(full quilt on page 63)

STACK IT UP AND OUT

The idea here is to embellish embellishments by stacking buttons, trims, appliqués, etc. for high textural and visual effect.

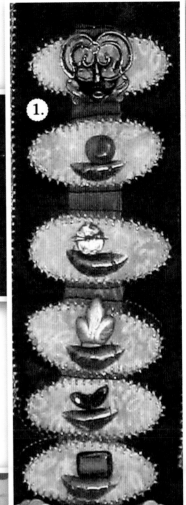

1. A single bead may be the best color but not big enough for the space. A solution is to stitch a mix of beads over fused appliqué shapes. Note that the colors blend for high textural effect. The mask is a pin.

2. A button may be the right color but the wrong shape. Here buttons are enhanced by stitching over blue iridescent crinkle sparkle organza.

3. Similar qualities of color and design in embellishments can add interest to a fabric without overwhelming it.

CONTEMPORARY CRAZY PATCH, 16" x 23", made by the author

TASSELS AND BEAD DROPS

Pretty things hanging down from an embellished work just make sense! Using some of the same elements in a quilt to make tassels or bead drops continues the theme of the quilt.

The bead drops shown are part of my DOMESTIC CATS quilt (page 34). It is so easy to make these little additions and they give some extra "oomph" to the work.

Simply lay out the beads and charms in an interesting configuration and string them together with beading thread. For the cherries I knotted the threads, added a leaf bead, knotted again, then added the cube. Be sure to leave enough thread to secure the embellishments to the quilt.

THE BASIC TASSEL

Follow this simple sequence to make a basic tassel.

1. Choose your yarn. This is a dyed-in-the-skein acrylic yarn from Red Heart Yarns. You can see that the two tassels in progress look different, but they were both wound from the same ball of yarn.

2. Wrap yarn around a piece of cardstock cut to the size you want.

Use a piece of yarn to tie off the top of the tassel. Use another piece of yarn to tie around the neck of the tassel to create a "head."

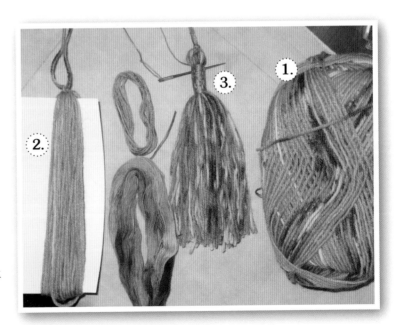

3. Wrap gold cotton yarn around the neck of the head. Use pearl cotton to make little stitches into the neck for added decoration.

INSPIRATION FOR A TASSEL

Nature is the inspiration for manmade tassels.

The dried sedum in my back yard is the inspiration for this tassel.
I love the shape of the seed heads.

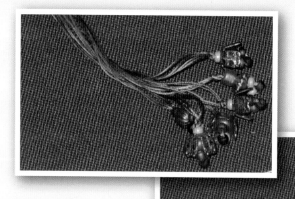

I gathered bead caps and beads and a multicolored brown
cotton thread that was perfect. Cotton thread is not the
preferred thread for beading, but this had the perfect
color, weight, and feel. I will be like sand sculptors and
not worry about the future.

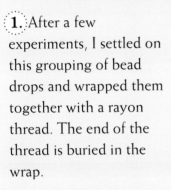

1. After a few experiments, I settled on this grouping of bead drops and wrapped them together with a rayon thread. The end of the thread is buried in the wrap.

2. Glue is applied to the loose threads and twisted, then set it aside to dry.

3. Big beads are strung onto the dried thread bundle and glued in place. The tassel is wrapped again with a contrasting thread that is also used as a hanger.

4. This photo shows the tassel in a project.

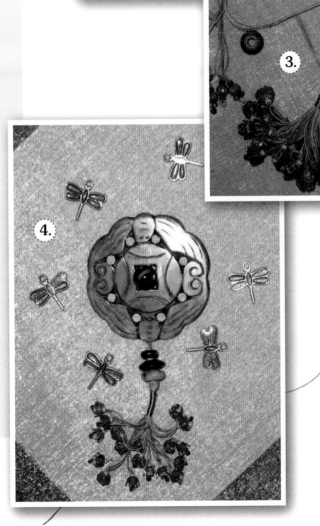

RASPBERRY TASSELS

This tassel is made with twisted cords.

1 strand each of Star cottons in light green, turquoise, and teal
2 strands of gold metallic thread
1 strand of bright green metallic thread

Cut 4 feet of each thread. Make the twisted cord according to the directions in String Theory (page 14).

Fold the twisted cord to make loops. Wrap the end of the loops with the gold thread. Secure by stitching through the wrap several times.

Thread a hand needle with 1 strand each of blue and green threads cut into 8″ strands.

Thread the raspberry bead and catch the center folds of the twisted cords. Thread the needle back through the bead and thread a small deep pink bead, then knot the thread.

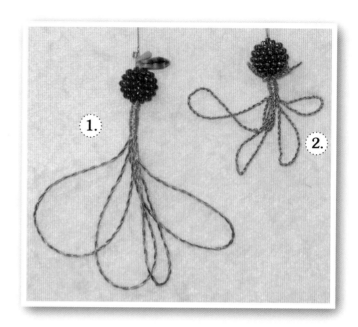

VARIATIONS:

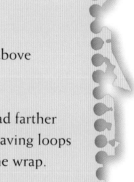

1. Use leaf beads above the raspberry.

2. Wrap gold thread farther down the loops, leaving loops on both sides of the wrap.

TASSEL CAPS

Every part of the tassel is an occasion for embellishment. I thought it would be great to make a cap out of a thimble. Hammer a nail in the top to make a hole. Then, thread the tassel string up through the hole to attach.

SPRING TOTEM began with the thread-painted moth, green doily, and the background fabric. The length of the quilt was determined by the length of the green rectangle lace trim. The process was a slow building of objects into a cohesive statement about springtime.

SPRING TOTEM, 15½" x 31", made by the author

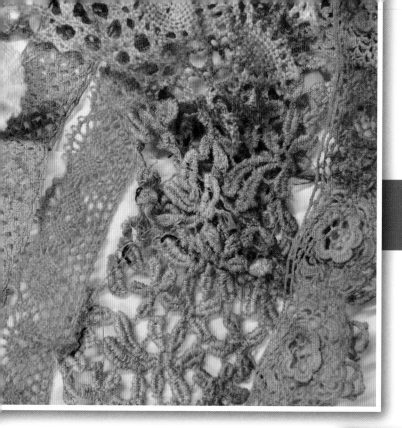

ALTERATIONS

Alter your embellishment to fit your desires!
Dye it, paint it, drill it, glue it, or wrap it!

For the quilt SPRING TOTEM (page 63), I painted the metal butterflies, a rubber snake, and plastic crayfish with acrylic paints. The lace pieces were hand-dyed, including the lace in the borders. The rickrack and lace clouds were painted.

White lace can be dyed or painted. The best way to know what works for you is to experiment with the many brands and types of both mediums. I like a combination of dying and painting lace to get a lot of wonderful effects. Follow the manufacturer's directions for each product.

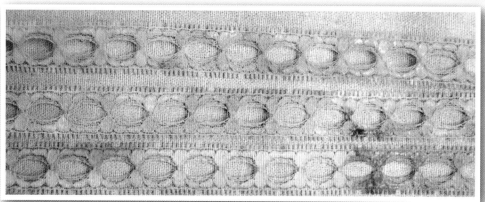

I painted this lace with diluted paint leftover from painting something else.

WOODEN SHAPES

I found this treasure trove of wooden shapes at a flea market for a only few dollars. You can buy them at craft stores.

1. I drilled holes in some of the shapes.

2. Then painted them with acrylic paints. The pin helped to hold the pieces still while I worked. They embellish NANA'S CLOUD BASKET (page 66).

3. I stitched the finished wooden pieces onto the work by hand. I used Artfabrik's hand-dyed pearl cottons (See Resources, page 93). Note the variety of stitching methods. The pin helped to hold the pieces while I worked.

NANA'S CLOUD BASKET, detail (full quilt on page 66)

NANA'S CLOUD BASKET, 11½" x 12½", made by the author

WRAP A BUTTON WITH THREADS

Three dull buttons are jazzed up with thread wrapping that totally changes their plain personalities!

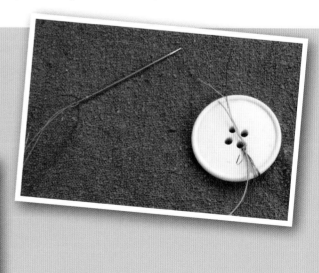

BIG FAN

BIG FAN, 22" x 18", made by the author

This quilt is a sampler of decorative stitches.
Several different feet and novelty threads were used.

SUN POPS

SUN POPS, 19" x 19½", made by the author

SUN POPS began with the desire to use the big shell and popsicle buttons. Once it looked like a sun, the dyed handkerchief came next. Then it looked like a landscape! The little girl showed up at the end.

ENHANCE YOUR QUILTS—EMBELLISH! • TERRY WHITE

HOLE IN THE SEA FLOOR

HOLE IN THE SEA FLOOR, 13" x 13", made by the author

This small work began with the yellow damask napkin and the zebra fish pin. There are holes in the sea floor that have unique ecosystems!

EMBELLISHMENTALITY

The examples in this chapter employ the techniques shown throughout the book. I wanted to present a mix of techniques with a variety of materials. You won't have the exact trims or beads that I have, but I hope this section shows you how to use the things you have. Some things are one-of-a-kind trims or buttons. Many are old things that I have collected over many years.

COLORS

1–1 A main color in this trim was matched with the color of the background cotton sateen. The stitches and thread colors used to enhance this trim mimic the colors and design in the trim. It "marries" the trim to the fabric.

1–2 One small bit of color in this trim matches the background fabric. The stitches bordering the trim are large geometric shapes stitched in colors found in the trim.

1–3 Here is an example of bringing disparate colors and designs together for a specific color theme. The coral fabric strip is fused to the green background fabric. The center trim is stacked on top with the rickrack on either side. The trims are temporarily glued in place with a glue stick. A hand-dyed pearl cotton is laid down on each side of the trim and rickrack, then bar tacked with a multicolor coral cotton thread. The bar tack stitches the trims together and to the stitch base. The repetition of the coral, blue, and green in the different materials makes an unusual trim.

1–4 The center is the same central trim used in 1–3. Here it is turned upside down for a completely different look. The stitch base is a purple hand-dyed fabric with a purple sparkle net overlay. The ball fringe is stacked on top and temporarily glued with a glue stick. The center trim is laid down and stitched along with the fringe to the stitch base with a buttonhole stitch using purple metallic thread.

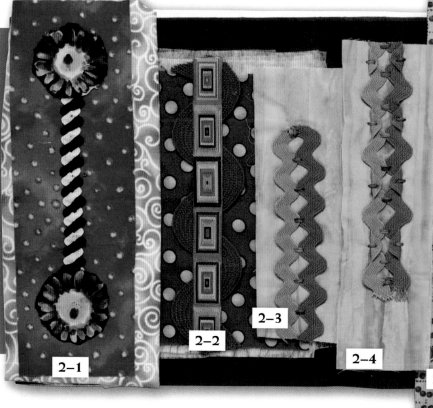

RICKRACK

2–1 The blue rectangle separates the trim from the background and enhances the colors. The pink and black flowers cut from fabric are fused and connected by a black-and-white rickrack twist. The pink in the background is repeated in the pink flowers and the rickrack trim repeats the black and white in the flowers.

2–2 This is a stack with a great trim on top of purple rickrack on top of a highly polka-dotted fabric. The colors in the trim bring the other elements together.

2–3 Two rickracks with a slight color difference, bar tacked together with a purple thread, make a simple design that allows the background fabric to show through.

2–4 Here is a variation of **2–3**. Alternate points on the rickrack are folded and bar tacked for a dimensional trim.

2–5 This is a big trim stack! It serves to join two different fabrics. Two shapes of green fabrics are fused and stitched to the stitch base with the same decorative stitch. Purple egg appliqué shapes are fused next. Then a green mini-rickrack is stacked with a light green jumbo rickrack and secured with a bar tack. Lastly, beads are stacked and hand stitched in place.

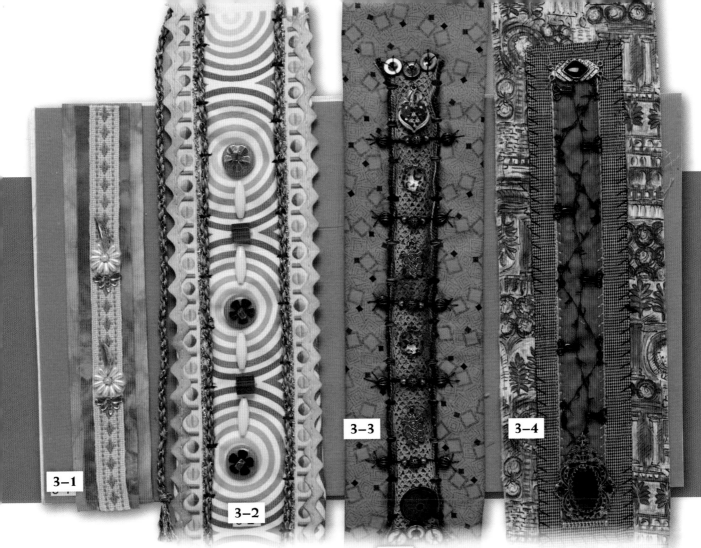

DISPARATE ELEMENTS

3–1 This trim stack starts with a fused strip of hand-dyed fabric onto the green stitch base. A woven trim is glued on top. Then, three disparate elements are applied with hand stitching to form a repeating motif. This is an artful way to extend a few small pieces while, at the same time, creating something entirely new.

3–2 VILLAGE FUNK will decorate the top of a hand bag. The Op Art fabric combined with the woven circle trim was the starting point for this piece. The pink rickrack matched the design of the circles perfectly and that doesn't happen every day! The hand-stitched beads are a mix of broken jewelry pieces, cheap beads, and flower sequins.

3–3 Lots of disparate elements are used in this trim. The control of color and materials used makes this trim an interesting art piece. The hand-dyed green lace is glued to the green print fabric stitch base. The greens contrast rather than "match." Strands of green hand-dyed pearl cottons and a textured black silk yarn are bar tacked with a black multicolor cotton thread along the sides of the lace. The additions are mostly mixed metals—brass, copper, and gunmetal colors. The hand stitching, which is done in a rust and black metallic thread, becomes part of the design. This trim will be used to decorate the spine of one of my turtle books.

3–4 The idea here started with the black hook and eye closures. As in **3–3**, colors and materials were chosen carefully. This trim includes velvet ribbon, broken jewelry, and a spring from a ballpoint pen.

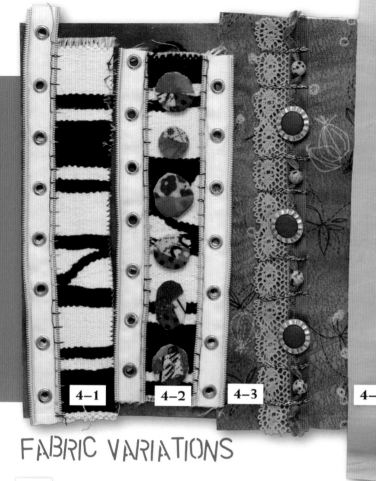

4–1 4–2 4–3 4–4 4–5

FABRIC VARIATIONS

4–1 Here is a black-and-white woven trim from Guatemala combined with an industrial-looking trim I found in a bargain bin at a fabric store. I once used this trim combination to join two large quilted panels.

4–2 Here is a continuation of **4–1**. The center "spots" were made by gluing fabric scraps to puffy foam, then cutting them into shapes and gluing to the trim.

4–3 Pink lace and rayon seam binding are glued to the brown print stitch base. Buttons and beads are strung onto a knitted tube yarn. A thin black-and-gold braid is laid down with big stitches crossing over the trim set, creating interesting divisions. The tube yarn is stitched down with lilac thread by hand using a cross-

stitch. The cross-stitch also tacks down the braid. The colors of individual elements are similar, but don't really match. This adds color interest.

4–4 Two strips cut from the selvage of a hand-dyed fabric are fused to the peach fabric stitch base, leaving a scant ½" space in between. The lace and blue twisted thread are bar tacked with gold metallic thread. The upper half of the lace is contrasted with the dark fabric and the lower half blends with the stitch base.

4–5 This rich trim from India is stitched with metallic thread onto purple netting, then overlaid on three different color fabrics to show the versatility of this kind of trim.

5–1 5–2 5–3 5–4

NOVELTY YARNS

5–1 Four strands of yarn are cut from a single ball of multicolor yarn and knotted. This can be glued and stitched to the stitch base.

5–2 Two motifs are made from a single ball of textured, multicolor yarn, coiled and glued to the stitch base. They could also be bar tacked or hand stitched in place.

5–3 Three strands of ½" wide ribbon yarn are bar tacked, looped, and bar tacked close to the loop base. A 1½" loop can be separated to make

what looks like three petals. A slight loop looks like a node on a branch.

5–4 The cherries are made from Red Heart® Spark-a-Doodle™ yarn—a thin twist with a pom-pom every 3". I used a metallic green thread to couch the stems with a zigzag stitch. The leaves are double-fused appliqué. The ribbon trim on the sides are two different polka dots with similar colors. This sample features a repetition of the circle shapes.

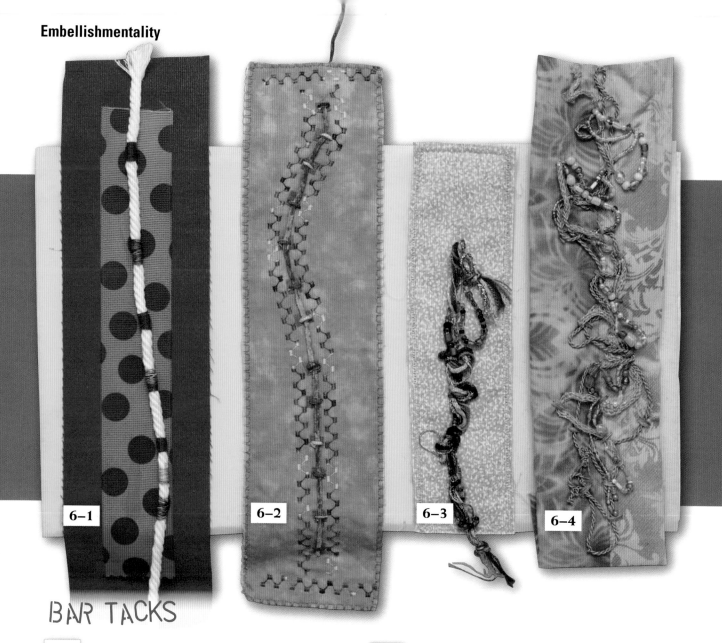

BAR TACKS

6–1 Wide orange with red polka dot grosgrain ribbon is glued to the red stitch base. The red color of the polka dots and the stitch base are very close, so it appears as if there are holes in the orange ribbon. White cotton upholstery cord is wrapped with cotton multicolor threads. A tiny bar tack in white thread attaches the cord to the center of the trim.

6–2 Orange hand-dyed chenille yarn is laid over fused squares of orange fabric, then bar tacked in place. The decorative stitches along the sides repeat the square motif. I like the yellow-to-orange color changes of the yarn, fabric squares, and thread.

6–3 Strands of pearl cotton, braided yarn, metallic cord, and a random bead string are knotted together at both ends. A bar tack is used to anchor the strands. Then the strands are twisted, knotted, and bar tacked. This is repeated down the length of the stitch base.

6–4 An extension of the ideas in **6–3**, this strand twist is stitched over the seam of two fabrics to soften the edge. Only one end of the strands is knotted. The strands are separated, bar tacked, overlapped, bar tacked, twisted and knotted, and bar tacked again. There are spontaneous and organic qualities to this treatment.

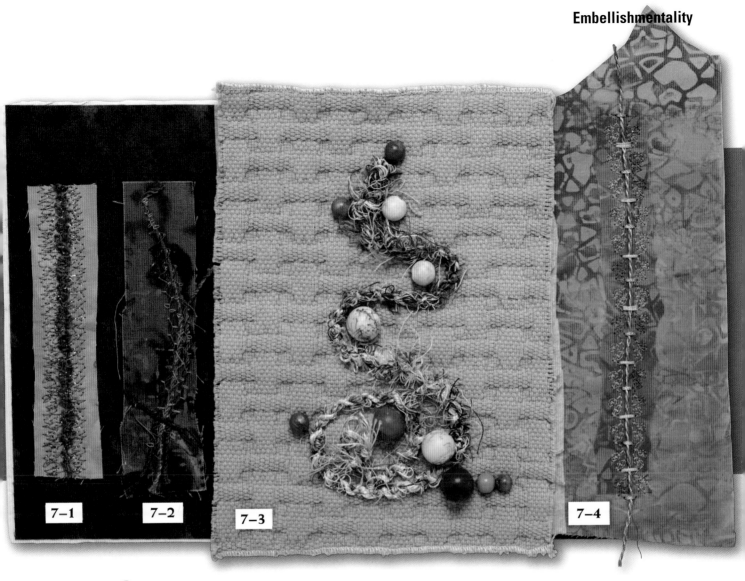

7-1 | 7-2 | 7-3 | 7-4

YARNS

7-1 A bulky yarn is overstitched with flat metallic purple thread in a random, open zigzag stitch. Two more rows of the same thread/stitch combination overlap the first stitching on either side. The same stitch is repeated with a flat metallic gold thread on the outsides of the trim.

7-2 Three strands cut from the same ball of hand-dyed silk yarn are stitched side-by-side with big, loose zigzag stitches. The same multicolor cotton thread is used in the bobbin as on the top, so when the bobbin thread is pulled up, the loops become part of the design. The look is achieved by a loose bobbin thread and a tight tension on the top thread.

7-3 This yarn was twisted from my thread compost using the Spinster tool. It is stitched to a cotton basketweave upholstery fabric.

7-4 An irregular strip of fabric was cut from a dark section of the stitch base and fused to a lighter section. I twisted threads with my bobbin winder to make the center cord. The same threads used in the twisted cord are used to stitch the cord with a bar tack and to stitch the leaves on either side.

8–1   8–2   8–3

ASSEMBLAGES

8–1 I call this little assemblage, ARTist. A woven clothing tag, with a word ending in "ist" was wandering around my work table and ended up next to the central button and the start of a Log Cabin block. I put the parts in a little clear bag, added some more parts, along with a needle, thimble, and thread. It was designed and assembled during a long car trip. The stitch base is two double-fused fabrics, so there was good stabilization. Each item is hand stitched with the simplest stitches. This little work showcases the minutiae and the message. This will decorate an art box.

8–2 ALL GOOD TURTLES GO TO HEAVEN The ideas in this assemblage could be used for the door of a sacred place or dream project. The fabrics used gold satin double-fused to a pink

cotton. Glued onto the gold is a buff-colored Ultrasuede. Stacked on top of this is a piece of green lace in between lilac organdy ribbon edged in a hologram glitter. I played with the arrangements of jewelry findings, cheap beads, a button that looks like granite, and a turtle charm. This type of design work is really fun for me. I think that the finished piece reflects the type of mood I was in during the design process.

8–3 IMAGINE THAT! CAT! Various fabrics are stacked and fused. The cat novelty button is threaded onto rickrack, which is glued to the stitch base. The cat's window ledge is a stack of five fused rectangles, adding textural interest and keeping the cat button from wobbling. The beads are hand stitched and the pin is pinned on the stitch base.

MORE ASSEMBLAGES

9–1 In ROCKING TREE, thread wraps of two threads each blend the colors of the threads from one bundle to the next. The bundles are made in several sizes for the tree shape. The thread bundles and beads are stitched to an Ultrasuede stitch base. Lace trim is glued to the edge.

9–2 Thread bundles are stacked and rotated to look like flowers and leaves. The stitch base is orchid Ultrasuede stacked with a hand-dyed lace. The cheap beads are glued in place. The assemblage is framed in strips with fabric cut from hand-dyed fabric.

9–3 Stacks of double-fused fabrics are cut into shapes and glued together to enhance the bow pin. The bead drops are made of beads from broken jewelry and knotted rayon cording. The drops are attached to the back of the shape with fused tacks.

9–4 This is simply a configuration of beads hand stitched onto a piece of Ultrasuede.

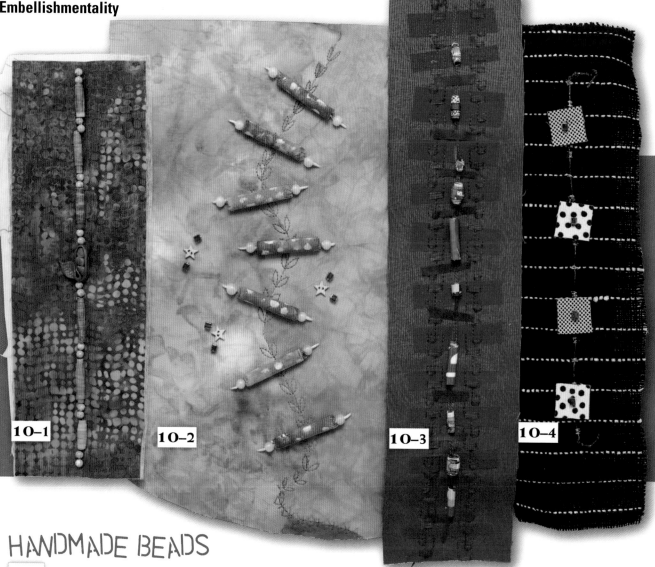

HANDMADE BEADS

10–1 Colored tracing paper beads are alternately stitched with round stone beads onto a batik fabric stitch base. This type of bead works well with the subtle coloring of the fabric. The central bead in this trim is a bean pod I made from FIMO polymer clay about 20 years ago.

10–2 The stitch base is made of two fabrics fused to a fusible interfacing, then stitched with a leaf pattern. The decorative leaf stitch was widened several times during stitching. Pink fabric beads are painted with yellow dots and handstitched to yellow plastic beads with yellow crochet cotton. The random bead groups of yellow star buttons and red square beads make an interesting allover surface design.

10–3 Deep red rectangles of fabric were fused onto the slightly lighter color red fabric stitch base. The red decorative stitching mimics the rectangles. Red fuse tape anchors the glossy magazine beads strung on red pearl cotton.

10–4 The black silk striped fabric used as the stitch base determines the size of the two-sided, fused felt square beads, each accented with red beads. The squares are strung with sparkle rayon deep rose cord, alternating which side faces up. The cord is stitched with random spurts of zigzag stitches of a rose flat metallic thread. This trim will be inserted between the main design and the border of a quilt.

PAPER BEADS

11-1 This large bead is made from a printed tissue paper found in a gift bag. The fabric scraps forming the stitch base were floating nearby as I was considering this bead. The additional beads are chosen for their color and form.

11-2 Beads made from an animal print gift bag are strung on a thread twist cord, knotted to secure the beads. The knots look like beads. The stitch base is a cotton print strip applied to a nubby silk weave with corded appliqué and decorative stitching. The coral threads in the cord and decorative stitches echo the coral color in the silk stitch base.

11-3 Beads made from a red advertising circular are strung and knotted on red pearl cotton along with clay pony beads. The stitch base is black wool felt.

11-4 The table of contents and some ads in a tourist guide provide the interesting type in these beads. They're strung in a formal arrangement. The stitch base is a lightweight wool suiting fabric, lending a business-like look to the sample.

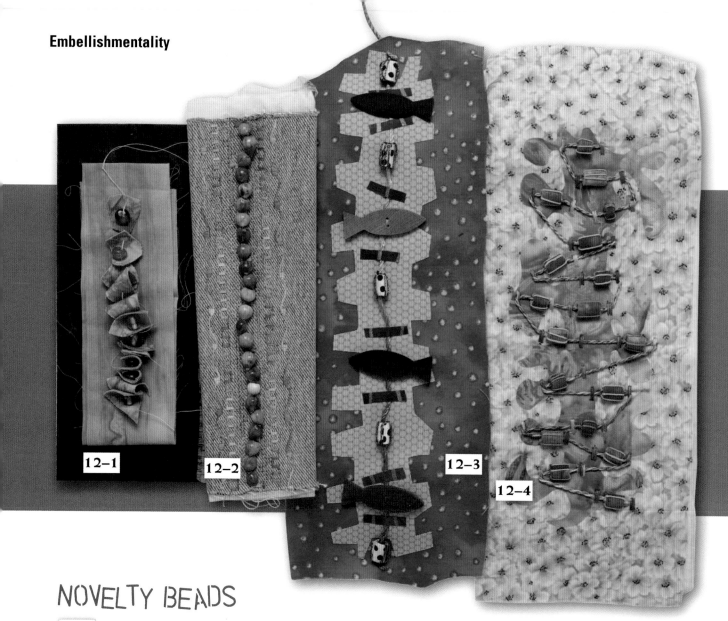

12–1   12–2   12–3   12–4

NOVELTY BEADS

12–1 Irregular shapes of double-fused fabric are strung with a mix of green glass beads. The stitch base has slivers of fused shapes as an allover design.

12–2 Decorative stitches in a multicolor taupe thread enhance the denim stitch base, cut from a pair of old blue jeans. The beads are actually seeds, strung and bar tacked in place. This panel could decorate a blue jean purse made from the same pair of jeans.

12–3 The green shape is appliquéd. Black polka dot fabric beads are wrapped with pink rayon yarn. The same rayon yarn is used to string the beads. The pink yarn repeats the pink in the blue background fabric and the black polka dots of the beads repeat polka dots in the fabric. The bead string is secured with fabric tacks made from dark green fabric. Using two different green fabrics adds depth of color. Red and orange fish buttons add a strong contrast. The green shape brings the disparate elements together and makes a strong design.

12–4 The stitch base is an irregular shape cut from blue hand-dyed fabric fused to a pink floral fabric. The beads are fabric beads wrapped with crochet cotton. The beads are strung on a twisted cord made with blue and pink threads and bar tacked with a pink multicolor thread.

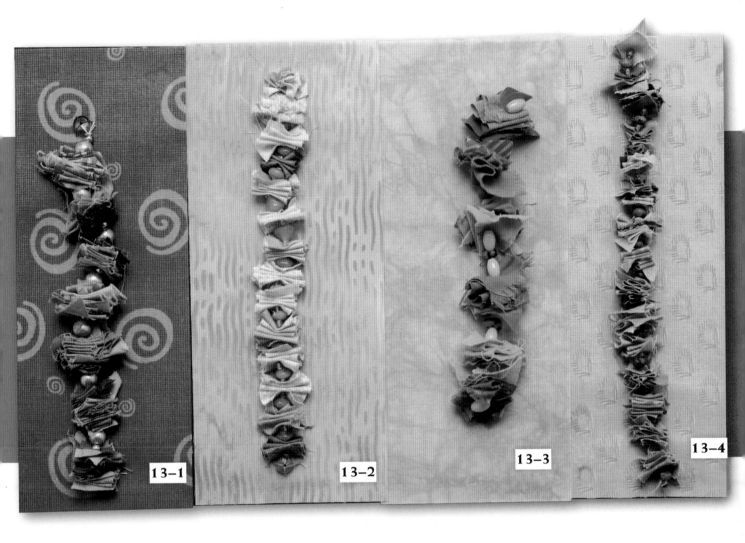

FABRIC SCRAPS AND BEADS

13–1 All the colors here create a rainbow effect. The scraps are irregular shapes that add to the unruly wildness of the beads. The alternating beads are silver spacers and natural color faux pearls from broken jewelry.

13–2 The pleats used to make the pink beads are very tight, resulting in a thin bead. The coral, pink, and mauve color mix of the fabrics creates more textural interest. The fabric beads alternate with a combination of pink rocaille beads and cheap pink plastic beads from broken jewelry.

13–3 Irregular shapes are used to make the mostly blue (with some green) fabric beads. They are strung alternately with cheap blue beads and faux turquoise beads.

13–4 Green fabric scrap beads are strung with green E beads and faux turquoise beads. The beads are repeated in a combination of green-turquoise-green between ½" scraps of fabric.

CERAMIC SPACERS AND FELT BALLS

14-1 The little white X's are spacers for laying ceramic tile. They are hand stitched with white pearl cotton on a very busy fabric stitch base. The closeness and repetition of shape and color make this an effective embellishment on the busy background.

14-2 Ceramic tile spacers painted with yellow paint are hand stitched with yellow pearl cotton. They alternate with fabric beads.

14-3 Wonderful felt balls are handstitched on a polka dot background with Laura Wasilowski's hand-dyed pearl cotton thread (See Resources, page 93).

14-4 Here the felt balls are stitched over fused shapes. The stitch base is a remnant of a pillowcase with a lovely crochet edging, hand-dyed by Judy Gula (See Resources, page 93).

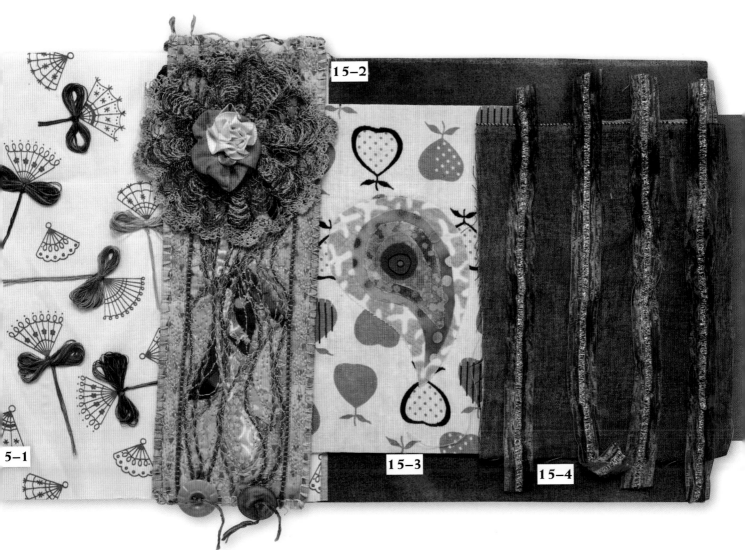

15–2

5–1

15–3

15–4

ALLOVER DESIGNS

15–1 The allover print fabric used as the stitch base is enhanced with thread bundles, stitched at the base of the fan design. The thread trails are glued with a good fabric glue.

15–2 An allover design is made with slivers of pink and purple fabrics, tacked down with glue onto the stitch base. Free-motion stitching with a pink rayon thread stitches down the slivers, leaving the edges to fray. Cords of sparkle rayon and pearl cotton are stitched down the length of the panel in wavy lines, using a cording foot. Turquoise embroidery floss is couched with gold thread and a buttonhole

stitch. The rosette is made of a thread-painted dahlia stacked with a yo-yo and a purchased ribbon rose. Pink decorative stitching finishes the sides of this cuff bracelet.

15–3 Fused and stacked appliqué creates a large allover design on a small allover design. Keep the shapes simple and this is an effective fabric embellishment.

15–4 Turquoise and silver ribbon are fused in rows onto a cotton/lame fabric to create a striped embellished fabric.

YO-YOS

16–1 A green yo-yo is stacked with an old glass flower button, a red wooden bead, and a red seed bead.

16–2 A blue cotton fabric is overlaid with green metallic net. Both fabrics are treated as one—cut into a circle shape and stitched together—to make this yo-yo. It is stacked with an old green glass bead.

16–3 EMPTY NEST SYNDROME illustrates the idea that when you finally have your empty nest, you get to decorate! The yo-yo is made with a fancy gold fabric, stacked with a "nest" made from thread compost and topped with an elegant old button.

16–4 Four yo-yos of different fabrics, including gold net, are stacked, offset, and stitched together. The stack is topped with an old brass button.

16–5 This flower starts with shapes fused onto the stitch base. The pink yo-yo is stitched down with two pink threads in big stitches, anchored by pink beads on the outer edges, to look like stamens. The flower is topped with an old pink button.

17–1   17–2   17–3   17–4

THREAD WRAPS

17–1 A bauble is made from an interesting colorful yarn. It is attached to the stitch base by bringing the wrapping string to the back of the stitch base with a needle. The stitch base is a fused red circle of fabric. The extra slivers create a dimensional motif that stands out on the very busy print fabric.

17–2 Five yarn wraps are tied together and the wrapping strings left to hang down. The stitch base is stacked with a crinkle metallic organza and pink rayon hem tape.

17–3 This bauble is stacked with a pink crocheted rosette and flanked with dyed shell beads. The stitch base is a stack of purple hand-dyed fabric, a rust print, gold net, and ribbon yarn.

17–4 The yarn wraps are made with a metallic ribbon and a rich glowing rayon yarn. The metallic ribbon is also applied to the metallic embroidered silk dupioni to create stripes.

TASSELS

18-1 This tassel is made with blue rayon thread and an old gold, flat metallic thread. Positioned around the thread wrap is a yo-yo of blue and gold woven rayon. Beads and buttons are strung on the tassel string.

18-2 This tassel isn't wrapped. Three lace medallions are strung on the tassel string.

18-3 This tassel is wrapped, but there is no tassel string and the yarn is left in loops. The beads that form the tassel cap are stitched through the wrapping. The last bead has a large enough hole to string it to a project.

18-4 A thimble punched in the top with a nail and a tack hammer serves as a tassel cap. This tassel isn't wrapped, but it is tied at the top and the ties are strung through the thimble, threaded through the beads, and secured to yarn under the tassel cap. The yarn is left in loops.

MORE TASSELS

19–1 The yarn used here is a random color change multicolor wrapped with gold embroidery floss, and embellished with hand-sewn seed stitches in a multicolor cotton thread. The tassel cap was overstitched with a bulky green yarn.

19–2 This tassel's yarn is a mix of jute, black silk, rayon, chenille, wool, and something fuzzy. Rayon cord is used as the wrapping and coral-dyed hemp ties the bead grouping for the tassel cap.

19–3 Here is a tassel made from a shiny nubby yarn. The wrap is blue rayon with gold thread loop stitched at the base for extra texture. The tassel is not tied and the loops are cut at the top. The beads for the cap were stitched to the wrap.

19–4 Only four loops of twist cord make this tassel. It is wrapped with gold thread. The tassel cap is a raspberry acrylic bead and is attached, along with the leaf beads, with the tie string.

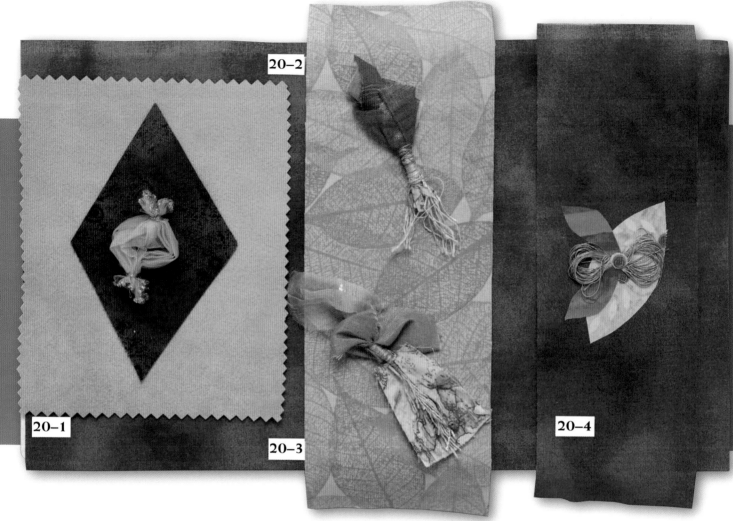

NATURALS

20–1 Wide wire-edge gold organza ribbon is pleated, drawn up and wrapped on the ends with green metallic thread, and hand-tacked to the stitch base of a cotton print fused to Ultrasuede. The variety in the textures of materials is as important as the colors chosen.

20–2 Three roughly petal-shaped fabrics are twisted and wrapped with a rusted cotton print and several novelty threads. The cotton is snipped into strips at the base of the wrapping and the threads are cut to different lengths. This embellishment looks like a strange budding plant that has been pulled from the ground with its roots intact.

20–3 Similar to **20–2**, the fabric shapes are wrapped with some threads in the center, so the threads look like stamens. The wrapping is stitched to a rust-dyed fabric with little pleats.

20–4 A thread wrap of metallic orchid and multicolor cotton is fused with a leaf-shaped fuse tack. The stitch base is a fused leaf shape cut from a green print on blue fabric. The stack is topped with a fused shape cut from the green print.

21-1 21-2 21-3

FUSED APPLIQUÉ

21-1 Double fused appliqué leaves are made from a hand marbled satin fabric (from *Quilter's Treasure*). The leaves fold over a highly textured novelty yarn. The yarn is shaped and stitched in an almost Celtic design.

21-2 Double-fused fabrics are cut into shapes and strips, glued to the stitch base, and handstitched with little beads. One shape is a scrap-stacked paisley.

21-3 Stacked scrap appliqué paisleys are humorous embellishments that I've used many times (see 15-3, page 85). They can be used in borders on clothing and quilts as well as used as an allover fabric design.

22–1

22–2

22–3

FABRICATIONS

22–1 Shapes are fused to a busy fabric print. Three strands of a roughly textured silk yarn are tacked over the shapes with beads and buttons. The buttons are wrapped with yarns. The busyness is controlled with color.

22–2 Print fabrics are fused to felt, stacked, and glued to make this small and highly graphic work.

22–3 Computerized embroidery design of a bug is fused to a hand-dyed fabric. Several colors of fabric markers are used to color in the white background of the embroidery. Multicolor cotton yarn is stitched over the fabric and couched with a tight zigzag stitch. The zigzag is stitched in small sections, alternating with sections of exposed yarn.

RESOURCES

Each of these websites not only has exquisite products, but also presents inspirational imagery!

April Melody

www.aprilmelody.com

Source for beautiful and unique world beads. Catch them at a quilt or bead show.

Artfabrik

www.artfabrik.com

Laura Wasilowski hand dyes the most beautiful fabrics and threads. I have been using her hand-dyed pearl cottons for umpteen years.

Artistic Artifacts

www.artisticartifacts.com

Judy Gula brings together the most unique grouping of charms, buttons, paints, and fibers to create the most beautiful embellishments. Her hand-dyed fiber collage kits were the basis for some of the projects in this book. This is a key place to go for gorgeous materials.

Cheep Trims

www.cheeptrims.com

Unbelievably beautiful and varied assortment of great trims and all the rickracks. info@cheeptrims.com

Cherrywood Fabrics, Inc.

www.cherrywoodfabrics.com

Quilters know Cherrywood fabrics! They are the beautiful, suede-look cotton, rayon, and corduroy fabrics. The colors are rich and perfect for embellishment work.

Coats & Clark

www.coatsandclark.com

The fresh new yarns are amazing. There are also free projects and inspiration on this site.

Creative Feet

www.creativefeet.com

An online resource for special machine feet.

Frieda Anderson

www.friestyle.com

Frieda dyes gorgeous fabrics. Her use of color in one yard of fabric is ingenious. There is so much coloration going on!

Havel's Scissors

www.havelsscissors.com

Good, sharp, precision scissors are important tools for embellishment work. These scissors are amazing!

Jeweled Treasures

www.JeweledTreasures.com

Carol is a Bead Princess! She has great style and her collection of beads and embellishments is just lovely.

Laura Murray Designs

www.lauramurraydesigns.com

Laura has beautiful clothing patterns—perfect for embellishments. Wonderful source for paints, kimono fabrics, and stencils.

Quilter's Fancy

www.quiltersfancy.com

Cindy Oravecz has a lovely assortment of braided trim, charms, buttons, embellishment fibers, and silks.

Rowan Yarn

www.knitrowan.com

Delicious, drippy, gorgeous yarns for embellishments are here. This website is like eating chocolate!

SewBatik

www.SewBatik.com

If you could eat fabric, this stuff would totally ruin your diet!

Spinster Cord Maker

www.ericas.com

Erica's Sewing site has lots of cool and fun-to-find notions.

Star Cotton Threads

www.starthreads.com

These beautiful threads are for machine embroidery, thread painting, quilting, and wrapping. This is also a source for free projects with videos.

Terry White

www.threadpaint.com

I sell my Beadle and The Strand Reel notions here, along with instructional CDs.

ABOUT THE AUTHOR

Terry coined the word "Embellishmentality" to describe a frame of mind and heart. It is the way in which a certain type of person sees things and makes things. It influences the way she designs her garden, decorates her home, and makes her art. Besides making her embellished textiles, Terry also creates art books, boxes, market bags, and jewelry. Everything she makes is one-of-a-kind and this work has always been a part of her life.

Photo by Liz Burgdorf

An avid "junker," she scours flea markets, thrift stores, and tag sales to find items to embellish or stuff to use as embellishments. Terry's family and friends know to give her their broken and junk jewelry because it will be transformed in her art.

Terry did not rest until she wrote this book of techniques. Hopefully it will be a source for quilters as well as clothing makers, crafters, costumers, doll makers, and creative home décor makers.

Currently, she is a BERNINA Artisan; she recently designed new multicolors for the Star Cotton thread line; and she is working on several projects for the Havel's Scissors website. Terry and her husband, Scot, produce video classes so everyone can learn her sewing machine-based techniques.

You can find Terry's tutorials and designs on YouTube and her blogs by going to her website www.threadpaint.com.

THIS PAGE: THE COLLECTION, detail. Full quilt on page 55.

MORE AQS BOOKS

This is only a small selection of the books available from the American Quilter's Society. AQS books are known worldwide for timely topics, clear writing, beautiful color photos, and accurate illustrations and patterns. The following books are available from your local bookseller, quilt shop, or public library.

#8240

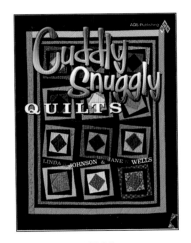

#8239

#8355

#8530

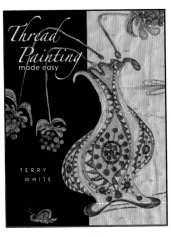

#7603

#8351

#8526

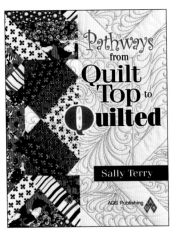

#8348

#8149

LOOK for these books nationally.
CALL or **VISIT** our website at

1-800-626-5420
www.AmericanQuilter.com